Introduction to LibreOffice Productivity Soft

Writer – Calc – Impress

By:

Darrell W. Hajek

Other books by Darrell Hajek

Computer textbooks:

Introduction to Computer Graphics

Introduction to Office Productivity Software: Word–Excel–PowerPoint

Introduction to Computers

(With Cesar Herrera)

Principles of Operating Systems

(With Cesar Herrera)

Fiction/Fantasy:

The Life and Times of Harry Wolf

The software suite LibreOffice provides an alternative to the widely used (but rather expensive) Microsoft Office suite. The fact that LibreOffice can be downloaded free should make it extremely attractive to a student just beginning to learn how to use a computer.

This book is intended for students with little or no experience with computers. It introduces the concept of a file, then describes how to utilize and navigate a file storage system. It gives brief descriptions and examples of how to use LibreOffice Writer, LibreOffice Calc and LibreOffice Impress.

It was written primarily in response to the increasing prices of the texts being used in laboratories supporting computer literacy courses. (The prices had increased to the point where students actively resisted purchasing them.) Another factor was the deteriorating support provided by the companies publishing those texts.

The aim of this book is to give a beginning student enough tools to make the programs (and his/her computer) useful. The book is intended as an introductory text, not a reference manual. After a student has begun using the programs, there are many resources (easily available) to help expand his/her capabilities as needed.

Contents

Introduction

1.1 What is a Computer

You might think of a *computer* as being principally for (numerical) *computing*[1]. In fact, though, computers are capable of, and are widely used for, much more than just numerical calculations. Computers are devices used for *information* processing.

The information that the computer processes can be organized in and stored as *computer "files"* and (usually) stored on some secondary storage device.

1.1.1 Computer Files

A **computer file** is a computer construct for recording and storing data in a computer storage device.

There are many different types of computer files. These different types of files are designed for different purposes. A file may be designed to store a picture, a written message, a video, a computer program, or any of a wide variety of other kinds of data. Some types of files can store several types of information at once (multimedia files.)

Files are given names to allow them to be identified. A "filename" will typically have two components, the file *name* and the file *extension*. These will be written in format: "*name*" then a dot then "*extension*"

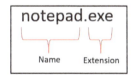

The extension normally identifies what kind of information is stored in the file.

Files with extension .exe (notepad.exe, blender.exe, …) will generally be computer programs that can be "*executed*".

Files with extension .txt (LabNotes.txt, shoppingList.txt, …) will normally be "*text*" files.

The program Microsoft Word will usually create files with extension .docx.

The program LibreOffice Writer will, by default, create files with extension .odt.

A file Created by the Calc program will typically have extension .ods.

A file Created by the Excel program will normally have extension .xlsx.

There are a large number of extensions in common use that identify many different types of data and/or different kinds of programs that created them.

Some kinds of computer programs can open, read, change, and/or close computer files, and the computer files can be reopened, modified, and copied any number of times.

Files are organized in a *file system*, which keeps track of where the files are located on disk and lets users (and/or their programs) find and access to them.

---

[1] There are still a few people like that around

1.1.2 File System

The file system keeps track of where on the storage device the files are stored.

Users identify the files by the "*filenames*". The files are organized in "*directories*"

A directory is a structure that can contain files and/or other directories.

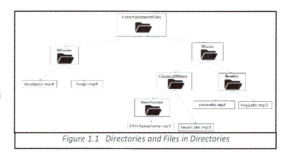

Figure 1.1   Directories and Files in Directories

(A directory contained in another directory is called a "*subdirectory*")

Directories are also given names and users can use those names to help identify the files contained in them.

Directory names are often chosen to identify what kinds of files they contain.

1.2 GUI

In order for *users* to "*use*" their computers, they must be provided a "*user interface*" for them to interact with. The most common kind of user interface is a *graphical user interface* (GUI).

In a graphical user interface, various elements in the computer system are represented by *icons*, (small pictures that can be displayed on the computer screen.)

These little pictures are often designed to give the user a hint as to what kind of element it represents.

Figure 1.2 Icons

Figure 1.2 Mouse

Chapter 1: Introduction

The user interacts with icons using a pointing device[2], most commonly a "mouse".

1.2.1 Mouse

When the user moves the mouse on a flat surface, the mouse senses the movement and causes a "pointer" on the computer screen to make corresponding movements.

The pointer is usually a little arrow

but it can take other shapes (,)
in certain situations.

A mouse will normally have (at least) two buttons.
If the pointer is *on/over/pointing at* an icon, then the user can use the mouse buttons to interact with the icon and/or the element in the computer system element represented by that icon.

There are a number of possible interactions:

Click: If the user "clicks" with the left mouse button (presses it and the releases it) the result will usually be to "select" the icon the pointer is pointing to. This will have the effect of marking the icon or associated system element for some use in the immediate future. Clicking on an icon also has the effect of deselecting any icons that had previously been selected.

Control Click: If the user has the keyboard's control key (CTRL) depressed while clicking on an icon, then that icon will be selected and any icons previously selected will remain selected.

Shift Click: If the user has the keyboard's SHIFT key depressed while clicking on an icon, then that icon will be selected and any icons between it and previously selected icons will also be selected.

---

[2] "Pointing" devices are devices that control the position of an associated "pointer" on the computer screen.

Double Click: If the user clicks twice in quick succession, the resulting action will depend on what kind of element the icon is associated with. If the icon is associated with an executable program, then double clicking on the icon will cause the computer to start executing that program. If the icon is associated with a file of a type that is usually dealt with by some specific program (a word processing program, a database manager, a browser ...[3]) then double clicking the icon will start that program running to deal with the file.

Right Click: Clicking (pressing and releasing) the right mouse button brings up a menu with additional options for whatever was clicked.

Drag: Holding down the left mouse button and moving the mouse will cause the icon to move to a new position on the screen.

Figure1. 3 Right Click Menu

1.2.2 Navigating the File System

We open the file window by clicking on the File Explorer icon in the taskbar.

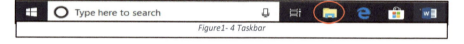

Figure1- 4 Taskbar

---

[3] Some file types frequently associated with specific programs include: .txt with Notepad, .docx with Microsoft Word, .xlsx with Microsoft Excel and .pptx with Microsoft PowerPoint

The file window is divided into three parts:

Ribbon[4]: Enables you to perform layout and formatting tasks

Navigation Pane: Used to access all kinds of locations: folders you've added to your favorites list, your libraries, the drives on your PC, and other PCs on your network.

Display Window: This is where the contents of the current folder or library are displayed.

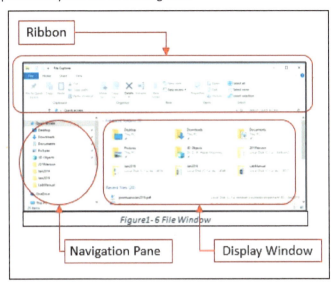

Figure1-6 File Window

Navigation Pane

Display Window

1.2.2.1 Ribbon

Figure 1-7 File Window Ribbon

The ribbon display will vary depending on several factors, but the primary factors will be the elements that are active and selected in the navigation pane and the display window.

Probably the most important element on the file system ribbon is the "New Directory" icon.

There are two copies of this icon, one located in the upper left corner of the ribbon, and the other approximately in the ribbon's center. Clicking on either of the icons will create a new directory.

Figure 1-8 Ribbon Illustrating New Directory icons

---

4 If the ribbon does not display, you can open it by clicking on the ∨ symbol at the right of the

toolbar

1.2.2.1.1 New Directories

New directories must be created in existing directories, so in order to use the
"New Folder" icon,
you must first have a
directory active in the
display window (for
how to activate a
directory in the
display window, see
1.2.2.2 below) to
serve as a parent
directory for the new
directory.

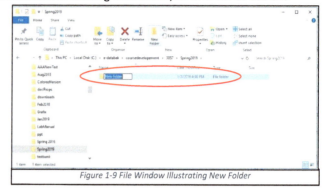

Figure 1-9 File Window Illustrating New Folder

Assuming that a directory is active, simply clicking on either of the *New Directory*
icons will cause a new directory with default name "New folder" to be created in
the active directory. The directory identification field is automatically active/open
for entry, and the user can simply type the name that he/she prefers and then
press the "Enter" key.

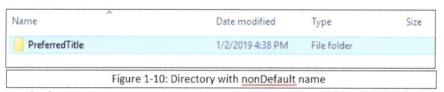

Name	Date modified	Type	Size
PreferredTitle	1/2/2019 4:38 PM	File folder	

Figure 1-10: Directory with nonDefault name

1.2.2.1.2 Deleting a Directory

If you want to delete a directory (or a file) navigate to
where its icon is displayed in the navigation pane
and/or in the display window.

Right click on the icon (place the cursor on the icon,
then press and release the right mouse button.)

A menu will open. One of the menu options is
"Delete"

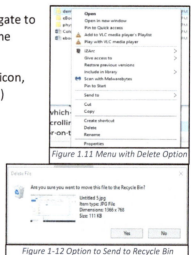

Figure 1.11 Menu with Delete Option

Click on the Delete option. You will be asked
whether you want to move the file or
directory to the recycle bin.
If you click on "Yes" and the file or directory
will be removed from the file system (to the
recycle bin[5].)

Figure 1-12 Option to Send to Recycle Bin

---

[5]   Items in the "recycle bin" can be returned to the file system. This gives the
       user a chance to later correct a deletion made by mistake. The recycle bin
       should be "emptied" periodically.

1.2.2.2 Navigation Pane

In the Navigation pane there will be a list of directory identifiers, most of which are

marked with the folder icon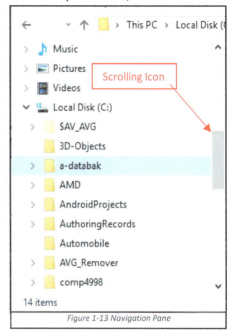

There will often be more directories than can be displayed in the navigation pane, so there will be a scrollbar on the right of the pane, and the user can change which directories are displayed by *dragging* the scrolling icon up or down (placing the cursor on the icon and then moving the cursor while holding the left mouse button down)

1.2.2.2.1 Directories and Subdirectories

Each directory has a name written to the right of the icon and some may have a right pointing arrow displayed to the left of the icon.

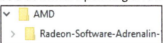

Such an arrow indicates that the directory contains other subdirectories.

Clicking on a right pointing arrow will cause the subdirectories to be displayed in the navigation pane. The subdirectories will be below the parent directory offset to its right. If a directory's subdirectories are being displayed. There will be a downward pointing arrow instead of a right pointing arrow.

If you click on a downward pointing arrow, the subdirectories will cease to be displayed and the downward pointing arrow will change to a right pointing

arrow

1.2.2.2.2 Selecting a Directory

If you *select* one of the directories in the navigation pane (by clicking on it) that directory will be identified by a blue band in the navigation pane, and the contents of the selected directory will be displayed in the display window.

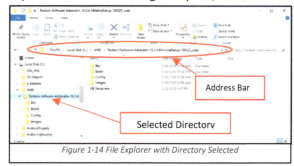

You can also select a directory by editing the contents of the Address Bar, located just above the display window.

Figure 1-14 File Explorer with Directory Selected

1.2.2.3 Display Window

The display window shows the files and subdirectories contained in the directory selected in the navigation pane

Figure 1-15 Illustration of Address Bar Position

These elements can be displayed in several different formats.

To control which display format will be used, you first click on the "View" tab in the ribbon.

Figure 1-16 Explorer Ribbon with View tab selected

Probably the most common formats are the "Details" format and the "Medium Icons" format.

1.2.2.3.1 Details Format

With the Details format, the files and directories are displayed each grouped together, each group as a list in alphabetical order. The directories displayed first and the files next. It also displays the date of

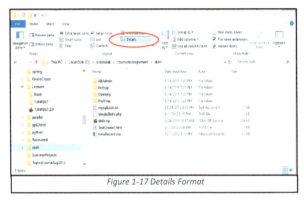

Figure 1-17 Details Format

the last modification of each, the type of element, and, in the case of the files, it indicates the sizes of the files.

1.2.2.3.2 Medium Icons Format

Using the Medium Icons format, the files and directories are represented only by (medium sized) icons representing the elements (together with their names.) Less information is displayed, but it is easier for a user to

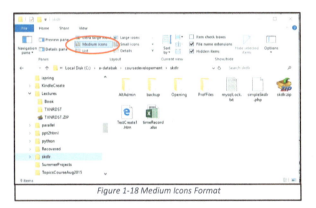

Figure 1-18 Medium Icons Format

select the element he/she might be looking for.

1.3   Notepad

Users must have some way of creating files to be stored in the directories of their file system. One of the simplest widely available programs for doing this is *Notepad*.

Notepad is a simple text-editing program provided with the Microsoft Windows system. It enables computer users to create and edit digital documents. The files created by notepad normally have a txt extension and are pure text files. They do not have hidden formatting characters (which can be problematic for applications such as computer programs.)

Figure 1-19 Notepad Icon

Notepad will normally be used for relatively short, simple editing tasks: (shopping lists, simple computer programs, notes, …)

Since it is so simple, it loads quickly. It does not have numerous editing options (which require extra time and attention when setting up a project and can be an extra source of confusion for a beginner.)

You open the Notepad program by clicking on the Notepad icon[6] 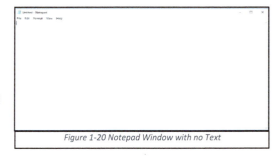. An empty Notepad window will open, at which point

Figure 1-20 Notepad Window with no Text

you can start entering text or can open an existing file to read, print and/or edit.

1.3.1 Using Notepad to Create a New Document

As just stated, with an open notepad window you can start entering text:

1.3.1.1 Adding new text

Text entry takes effect at the position of the notepad data cursor (typically a blinking vertical line.). After some text has been entered, you can change the position of the data cursor by using the arrow keys to move it up, down, left or right. You could also simply place the mouse cursor where you want the data cursor to be and then click with the left mouse button. When the data cursor is in the position where you want to insert new text, just start typing.

1.3.1.2 Deleting text

If the notepad window contains text that isn't wanted, you can delete it. Pressing the DEL key will delete the character at the right of the data cursor. Pressing the "Backspace" key delete the character at the left of the data cursor.

You can also delete text by first *selecting* a section and then pressing a key. The selected section will be deleted and, if the key pressed was that for a character to be displayed, the selected section will be replaced by that character

---

[6] Found under "Windows Accessories" in the menu obtained by clicking on the ▦ icon at the lower left corner of the screen.

1.3.1.3 Selecting by dragging

You can select a section of text by placing the mouse cursor at the beginning of the desired section, pressing the left mouse button and dragging the cursor to the end of the desired section and releasing the mouse button. The selected portion will be displayed with darkened background (as in Figure 1-21)

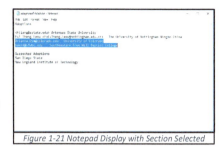

Figure 1-21 Notepad Display with Section Selected

1.3.1.4 Selecting by "Shift Click"

You can also select a section by placing the data cursor at the beginning of the desired section, then moving the mouse cursor at the end of the desired section, press the shift key and clicking with the left mouse button.

1.3.1.5 Editing: Copying, Cutting and Pasting

When a section of text has been selected, you can click on the Edit tab to display a menu and select any of several options(Figure 1-22)

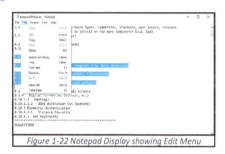

Figure 1-22 Notepad Display showing Edit Menu

(The actions available from the edit menu are also available using "short cut" key combinations without bothering to open the Edit menu)

Copy: will *copy* the selected contents to the *Clipboard[7]*.
   CTRL-C (hold the CTRL key down and press the C key)

Cut: will *cut* the selected section out of the document, i.e. copy the selected contents into the Clipboard and delete the selected section from the document.
   CTRL-X (hold the CTRL key down and press the X key)

Paste: will copy the contents of the clipboard into the document If a section of text is selected, the contents of the clipboard will replace the text in the selected section. If no text is selected, the clipboard contents will be inserted into the document at the location of the data cursor.
   CTRL-V (hold the CTRL key down and press the V key)

---

[7] The *clipboard* is a section of memory where data can be stored in order to later transfer (copies of) that data to other locations in a notepad file. It can also be used to copy that data into other notepad files or other applications (Word or Writer documents, Excel or Caslc files, etc.)

1.3.1.6 Editing: Searching and Replacing

When working with a large document, you will often want to find a place where a particular word or phrase occurs.

The Editing menu provides two tools to support this type of operation.

Find: Will search (either downward or upward) through the document to find an occurrence of text chosen by user and place the data cursor where it is found. The user must, of course, see to it that the text being sought is in the text box in the dialog box that appears.
CTRL-F (hold the CTRL key down and press the F key)
(Figure 1-23)

Figure 1-23 Notepad Display with" Find" dialog box

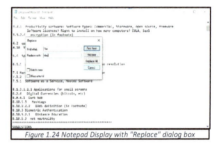

Replace: Will search (either downward or upward) through the document to find an occurrence of text chosen by user, will place the data cursor at that location and will replace that text with different text. The user must, of course, see to it that the proper text strings are entered in each of the text boxes in the dialog box that appears.
CTRL-H (hold the CTRL key down and press the H key)
(Figure 1-24)

Figure 1.24 Notepad Display with "Replace" dialog box

1.3.1.7 Saving a Notepad Document as a File

When a document has been edited into the form that you want it, then it should probably be saved to disk for some future use.

Notepad offers two options for saving a document. If you click on the "File" tab, a menu will appear showing options (Figure 1-25):

Figure 1-25 Notepad Display of File Menu

"Save" Which will save the document, in its current form, with the current name, replacing the version of the document with that name currently on the disk. Use of this option assumes that the current document has been assigned a name and is associated with an earlier version of the document which is stored on disk. The same thing is accomplished by pressing CTRL-S while in normal document display.

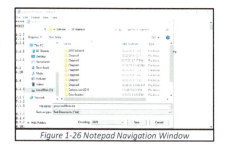

Figure 1-26 Notepad Navigation Window

"Save as" Which will open a navigation window. You can use this window to select a directory where the file will be stored, and then you can enter a file name for the document. (Figure 1-26)

1.3.2 Using Notepad to Open an Existing File

To open an existing file from the notepad window, you click on the File tab and select "Open" from the menu that appears(Figure 1-27) This opens a dialog box similar to the file window, with a navigation panel and display window (Figure 1-28) You can use the navigation panel to navigate and select directories (the path to the selected directory will be displayed in the address bar.) By default, the display window shows directories and .txt files in the selected directory (Figure 1-29)

The types of files that will be displayed can be changed by changing the setting in the document display type box. The alternative setting is *.* which will result in *all* files in the selected directory to be displayed (Figure 1-30).

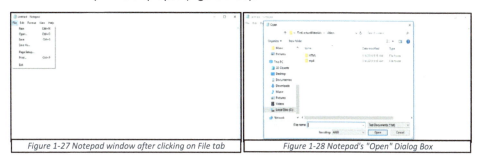

| *Figure 1-27 Notepad window after clicking on File tab* | *Figure 1-28 Notepad's "Open" Dialog Box* |

If one of files is selected, then its name will be displayed in the "File name" box beneath the display window.

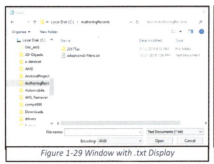

Figure 1-29 Window with .txt Display

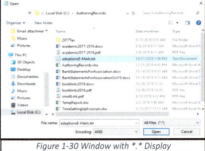

Figure 1-30 Window with *.* Display

When you have selected a file, you can click on the "Open" box/button. The selected file will open in the Notepad window and you can view and edit the contents of the Notepad document.

1.3.3 Opening a Notepad Document from the File System Window

You can also open notepad documents directly from the file system window.

You double click on an icon representing a .txt file. In this case a Notepad window will open and the content of the file will display in the window.

You might also right click on a file icon (not necessarily a .txt file.) The menu will open. You would select "Open with" from the menu and, from its submenu find and click on "Notepad" (See Figure 1-33) A Notepad window would open and the content of the selected file would display.

1.3.8 Printing a Notepad Document

The File menu also includes an entry for printing the document. If you click on this entry, the print dialog window will open.

This window allows you to select the printer to be used, as well as the number of copies to print and other printing factors.

Pressing CTRL-P while in document display will print the document directly on the default printer.

Figure 1-31 File Open in Notepad

Figure 1-32 File Directory with .txt File

Figure 1-33 Illustration of "Open with"

Figure 1-34 Notepad Print Dialog Window

1.3.9 Closing a Document

When you have finished working on a document (and have saved any information you will want to reference later and have done any printing you want to have done) you should close the document window.

There are two ways you could do this.

1. Open the menu under the File tab and click on "Exit"

2. Click on the x in the upper right corner of the window. (This will close most windows in Microsoft Windows system).

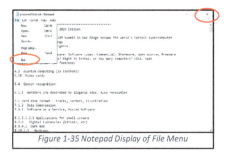

Figure 1-35 Notepad Display of File Menu

1.3.10 Notepad Help

Like most Microsoft applications, the Notepad window includes a "Help" tab

Since Notepad was designed to be simple and use very few resources, the application itself does not include any actual help information. The "View Help" option is a link to online resources, which are, of course, quite extensive. They do, however, require Internet access.

1.4 Accessing the Internet

One of the main uses of computers today is to access the Internet, and most commonly, the World Wide Web. You access the World Wide Web using a program called a *browser*. There are a number of different browsers, but most of them share common features.

The browser we will discuss here is called Microsoft *Edge*.

1.4.1 Internet Addresses

The Internet consists of a large number[8] of computers and communications devices, all of which are interconnected in a huge communications network.

Each site in this network is identified by an IP address (a combination of four numbers separated by dots or periods e.g. 72.21.211.176) Many of the sites (the ones we are generally most interested in) are also assigned a text identification called a *uniform resource locater* (more commonly referred to as a URL. Also sometimes referred to as a uniform resource *identifier* or URI.)

A typical URL could have the form   *(protocol)://(hostname)/(filename)*

---

[8]   a *REALLY* large number

Example: http://www.example.com/index.html ,

this illustrates a *protocol* (http), a *hostname* (www.example.com), and a *file name* (index.html)

It is common to specify URL's without identifying a protocol (in which case the default protocol http or https will be used) and/or without specifying a filename (in which case a default file name will be used, often index.html)

Examples of URL's:

https://mail.google.com/mail/u/1/#inbox
http://correo.upr.edu/
ftp://ftp.gnu.org/

1.4.2 Opening the Browser

When you want to access the World Wide Web, you would start by executing a program called a *browser*. You click on the appropriate icon

, a window will open with displaying the Web page from a default URL. (See Figure 1-36)

Figure 1.36 Edge Browser with display from www.google.com

You *can* get a new Web page, change the display in the browser window by entering a URL in the address bar. (Figure 1-37 shows, most browsers will show suggested URL values as we type.)

Figure 1.37 Edge Browser with (partial) URL Entry in Address Bar

It is much more common, however, to open a display in the browser window by clicking on a link in the browser display window. A *link* (more precisely a *hyperlink*) is a object (a section of text, or an image) that is associated with another Web item (most commonly a Web page.) When you click with the cursor pointing to a *link*, the browser will attempt to retrieve and display the item associated with that link.

You can tell if the cursor points to a link because then it will have the form of a finger. If the cursor is pointing to a link (which can be a section of text, as in figure 1-38 or it can be an image.)

Figure 1-38 Edge Browser with Cursor pointing to Link

1.5 E-Mail

Email is a system for exchanging messages by means of the Internet and is one of the oldest services provided by the Internet.

Today's email systems are based on a "store-and-forward" model. That means, when a user sends an email message, it gets "stored" in an account on an email "server" and remains there until the intended recipient logs into that account and downloads the message. The sending user and the destination user do not have to be online at the same time. Each needs to be online only for as long as it takes to send or receive the message.

Chapter 1: Introduction

There are many email servers. Some of the better known are yahoo, hotmail and gmail. Most companies of any size have e-mail servers for their employees to use. Schools often have e-mail servers for their faculty and students.

Figure 1-39 gmail user window

To access your email messages, you enter the url of the server (see figure 1-37 above), then identify the email account

(john.smith28@gmail.com, juan.garcia12@upr.edu, …),
You enter the password for the account and the user window will open, displaying messages that the account has received. Clicking on one of the entries will open that message and display it in the email window.

Figure 1-40 gmail user window with open message

The first email systems could only handle text messages, but now emails can contain multimedia (images, sound and videos) as well.

You can also use the email system to send your own emails. In order to send an email from the gmail system, you begin by clicking on the "+ Compose" symbol in upper left part of the gmail window. A "New Message" window will open.

You can type text directly into the New Message window or you can copy text or graphics from the clipboard into the New Message window.

You can also use the New Message control bar

Figure 1-41 gmail user window with New Message window

to insert photos into the message

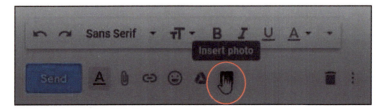

to insert contents of a file from the cloud

to insert an emoji

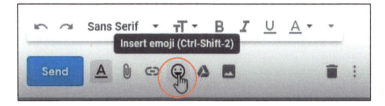

to insert a hyperlink

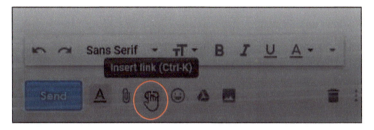

to attach a file to be sent along with the message

1.6 E-Mail Example:

In this example, we will illustrate how you might use email to send a recipe to a friend.

1.6.1 The recipe ingredient list in Notepad

The list of ingredients for the recipe is a little long Figure 1-42.) It will be better to compose the list "offline" using a program designed for text editing (Notepad for example) and then copy it into the New Message window. Using a text editing program, it will be easier to correct errors, make substitutions, modifications, etc.

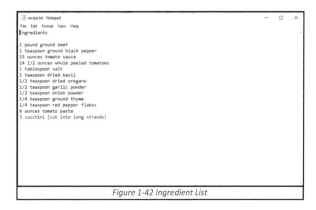

Figure 1-42 Ingredient List

1.6.2 Starting the Email

Open the "compose message" email application, enter the email address of the intended recipient and enter a brief message for him/her.

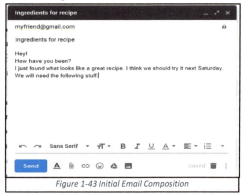

Figure 1-43 Initial Email Composition

1.6.3 Inserting the Ingredient List

Copy the list of ingredients into the clipboard (select, then CTRL-C) and paste it (with CTRL-V) into the composition window.

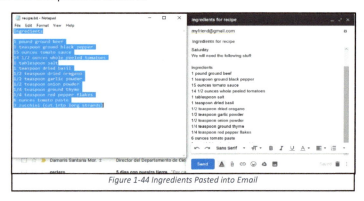

Figure 1-44 Ingredients Pasted into Email

1.6.4 Attaching Picture

You might also want to "attach" a picture of the dish. Click on the "Attach file" icon 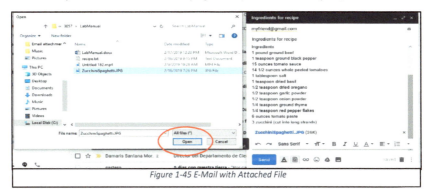 and, when the selection window opens, navigate to the directory with the image, select the file with the picture of the ZucchiniSpaghetti and click the "Open} button

Figure 1-45 E-Mail with Attached File

1.7 Exercises:

1.7.1 Exercise 1

Create and send an email with a list of at least 5 names and phone numbers

1.7.2 Exercise 2

Create and send an email with a photo of yourself attached

1.7.3 Exercise 3

Create and send an email with a recipe. The body of the email should include a list of ingredients (as in example 1.6) A text file with the preparation instructions should be attached to the email.)

Word Processing

2.1 Introduction to LibreOffice Writer

As mentioned earlier, Notepad is a good program to use for the creation of short simple documents with only text and no complex formatting. For bigger projects a more complex program is needed. One of the most widely used word processing programs is Microsoft Word. The LibreOffice alternative is named "Writer"

To open the Writer program, you simply click on the "LibreOffice Writer" icon  and a Writer window will open (Figure 2-1.)

Figure 2-1 Initial Writer Window

The Writer window includes a toolbar along the top.

This toolbar has a number of icons which provide quick and easy access to several commonly used word processing activities.

In addition, there are several named tabs along the top of the toolbar. Clicking on one of these tabs will result in a dropdown menu, giving access to even more word processing activities.

A few of these dropdown menus are shown below.

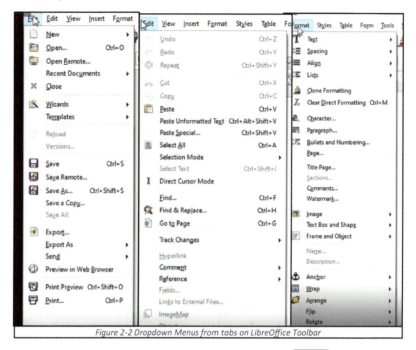

Figure 2-2 Dropdown Menus from tabs on LibreOffice Toolbar

You can initiate a new document by clicking on the "New" icon Clicking on this icon will open a new window similar to that displayed in Figure 2-1

If, instead of beginning a new document, you want to edit an existing document, then you

click on the "Open" icon. This opens a navigation window, and you can search out the desired file

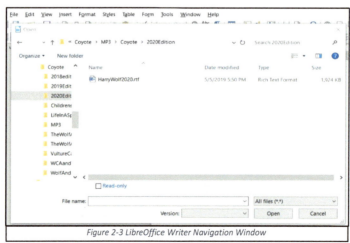

Figure 2-3 LibreOffice Writer Navigation Window

Select the desired document and click on the "Open" button

and a window will open, displaying the document for editing.

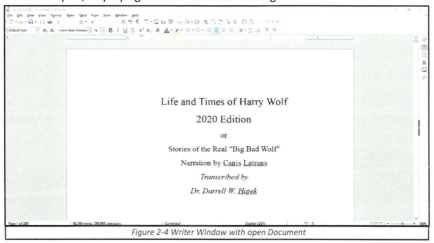

Figure 2-4 Writer Window with open Document

The default file type for Writer documents is .odt but it also handles .txt, .docx, .rtf and many others.

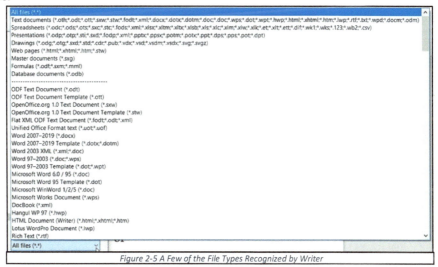

Figure 2-5 A Few of the File Types Recognized by Writer

2.2 Writer Example 1: Job Application

In this example project, we will illustrate several of the writing/editing tools of LibreOffice Writer by describing the construction of a letter that might be written by a job applicant.

In order to start the example document, we open the LibreOffice Writer program 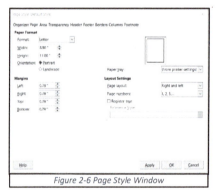, and, as described above, the program displays a blank editing screen (as in Figure 2-1.) It is not necessary to click the "New" icon, we can simply begin editing the default blank document.

2.2.1 Paper Size and Margins

It will probably not be necessary very often, but you can adjust the page size (the height and width of the paper that the document would be designed to be printed on) and the widths of the margins. These controls can be found by clicking the "Format" tab in the toolbar and selecting the "Page" option in the dropdown menu.

Figure 2-6 Page Style Window

This will open a the "Page Style window where page dimensions, the margins and orientation

(portrait  or landscape) can be adjusted.

2.2.2 Non-Printing Characters

In the initial (blank) editing screen you will see a blinking vertical line identifying the insertion point of the document. You *might* also see the ¶ symbol beside the blinking line. There will probably be a mouse cursor somewhere on the screen as well.

The ¶ symbol is a "*paragraph marker*" a *non-printing* character (more about non-printing characters shortly) and the blinking line is the *insertion pointer*. The insertion pointer marks the position where our data entry will take effect. Your system can be configured to display the ¶ symbol by default, or not to display it.

Non-printing characters, or **formatting marks**, are characters identifying content *design* in word processors. They aren't displayed at printing. They control the *format* (the way that text is displayed or printed) but do not result in any output themselves. The most common of the formatting marks are:

¶   paragraph break

·   single space

→   tab

↵   line break

Many people do not like to have the formatting characters displayed while they are editing, preferring to see their text "the way it would look".

You can enable or suppress the display of the formatting characters. clicking on the ¶ icon in the toolbar.

This will toggle between enable and suppress display formatting marks.

For our example, we will enable the display of formatting characters.

As we type, the characters appear at the point marked by the insertion pointer. When we press the "Enter" key, a "paragraph break" marker (¶) will be inserted entered. If we press "Ctrl-Enter" a "line break" character (↵) would be entered.

You will notice in the example in Figure 2-7 that each line ends with the symbol¶ and that the different words are separated by a dot. These are non printing characters (formatting markers).

Figure 2-7 Example Letter

2.2.3 Paragraph Alignment

You will note that, in our example, the first four lines, identifying the name and address of the person sending the letter, are all positioned at the left of the page. Names and addresses of this kind are more traditionally located in the center of the page.

In order to position this text in the center of the page, first *select* the text to be repositioned (place the mouse pointer at the beginning of the text and left click, then place the pointer at the end of the text, hold the shift key down and left click. The desired text should be highlighted. Figure 2-8)

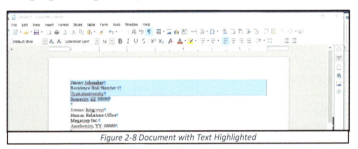

Figure 2-8 Document with Text Highlighted

Next find the "Center Content" icon in the toolbar. When you click on this icon, its background will change to a darker shade, and the selected text will move to center of the page (Figure 2-9).

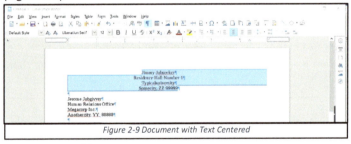

Figure 2-9 Document with Text Centered

2.2.4 Font Face and Font Size

It is common to display the "return address" at the top of a letter and to use text with a different appearance than that of the text in the rest of the document.

To change the "font face" of a section of text we select that section and then, in the Home ribbon, click on the ˅ symbol in the font section and, in the menu that appears, we you scroll down to the appearance we prefer and select that font (Figure 2-10)

Figure 2-10 Selecting Font Face

In the font section of the Home ribbon you can also adjust the size of the text

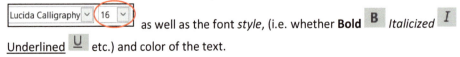 as well as the font *style*, (i.e. whether **Bold** **B** *Italicized* *I*

Underlined U etc.) and color of the text.

2.2.5 Date

It is customary to include the date of a letter, and the date will generally be located at the right margin of the document (right justified, rather than left justified, as the bulk of this letter, or center justified, as with the return address.)

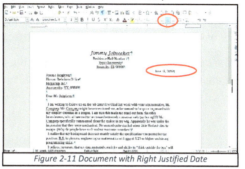

Figure 2-11 Document with Right Justified Date

2.2.6 Saving the Document

When you have finished the document (or simply want to stop, and continue editing later) you can save it to secondary storage.

If you are working on a document that had been saved before, then you can save the updated version by simply clicking on the "Save" icon in the upper left corner of the screen[9].

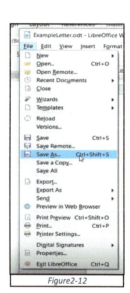

Figure2-12

If you have not saved the document before, you will initiate the "saving new document" process by clicking on the *File* tab and then selecting the *"Save As"* option from the list of options in the page that appears (Figure 2-12)

This will open the "Save As" window (Figure 2-13). In this window you can enter a name for the document, choose a directory in which it should be stored, and, if desired, choose a file type.

Figure 2-13 "Save As" Window

---

[9] It is recommended that this be done at regular intervals if you are doing extensive editing. It can be very frustrating if the computer suddenly stops working and you lose the results of a lot of work.

2.2.6.1 Document File Formats

Although LibreOffice Writer supports many different file formats, five of these formats are especially widely used.

.odt   An ODT file is a text document created by various word processors, notably, the Writer program included in Apache OpenOffice and LibreOffice. It contains different elements such as text, images, drawn objects, and styles.

.docx   This is the default format for Microsoft Word the docx format should be preferred if the document will be reviewed and/or re-edited using Microsoft Word. If, however, a document is stored in docx format, viewing it or editing it using another program can be problematic.

.pdf   This is a file format developed by Adobe in the 1990s to present documents, including text formatting and images, in a manner independent of application software, hardware, and operating systems. A document stored in pdf format will generally require less storage space than a docx document producing similar appearance. This format was designed to reproduce the appearance of the documents, not to facilitate editing of documents.

.rtf   This is a file format that will include all of the formatting controls (non-printing characters) in the document. Most word processors can read and write rtf formatted files. This format would be a good choice for a file intended to be shared with other people who might be expected to make modifications and who might not be using LibreOffice Writer or Microsoft Word. A file in rtf format will generally be larger than a similar file in .odt or .docx format.

.txt   A TXT file is a standard text document that contains unformatted text. It is recognized by any text editing or word processing program and can also be processed by most other software programs. TXT files are useful for storing information in plain text with no special formatting beyond basic fonts and font styles. The file is commonly used for recording notes, directions, and other similar documents that do not need to appear a certain way.

2.2.7 Paragraph Indentation and/or Spacing

Within the body of a document, there are two traditional ways to separate paragraphs: *indentation* and *spacing*. These are not the *only* alternatives, but they are by far the most common.

You can control these characteristics of your paragraphs (as well as several others) by first selecting the paragraph(s) you want to format, then clicking on the "Format" tab and then selecting the "Paragraph" option in the resulting dropdown menu (Figure 2-14).

Figure 2-14 Format Menu

When we click on the "Paragraph" option, a dialog window opens that allows us to adjust line and paragraph spacing and indenting

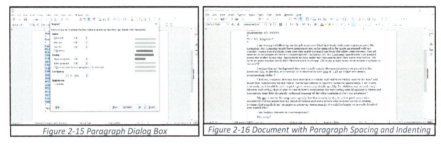

Figure 2-15 Paragraph Dialog Box	*Figure 2-16 Document with Paragraph Spacing and Indenting*

2.2.7.1 Paragraph Spacing

The paragraph dialog window allows you to require each affected paragraph to have blank space above and/or below it. How much space should be used will depend on the size of the text in the paragraphs, larger text requiring more space to signal the beginning of a new paragraph.

2.2.7.2 First Line indentation

As an alternative to putting extra space between paragraphs, you might choose to indent the first line of each paragraph.

First line indentation was commonly used when manual typewriters were common, and fine control of the vertical positioning of text was relatively difficult. It is not so common now. Combining paragraph spacing and first line indentation is considered overkill (one of the many things that our fictional Jimmy Jobseeker does not seem to understand.)

2.2.9 Exercises

2.2.9.1 Write a letter that Mr. Jobgivver might send to Mr. Jobseeker in response to his application. Save the letter/document as a .docx file. Create an email with the letter as an attachment.

2.2.9.2 Write a letter addressed to an academic administrator protesting a grade. Save the letter/document as a .docx file. Create an email with the letter as an attachment.

2.2.9.3 Write a letter addressed to a credit card company requesting a charge that appeared on your statement be cancelled. Save the letter/document as a .docx file. Create an email with the letter as an attachment.

2.3 Word Example 2: Second Letter

If a document has been saved, it can be re-opened later for re-editing.

In our example, if Mr. Jobseeker receives no response to his application (previous section) he might decide to send a followup, and, having a copy of his earlier letter with names and addresses already in place, he might start his followup letter by editing a copy of the earlier letter, rather than entering everything again.

He can open the existing document by first clicking on the folder icon in the taskbar and, in the dialog box that opens, navigate to the directory with the desired file.

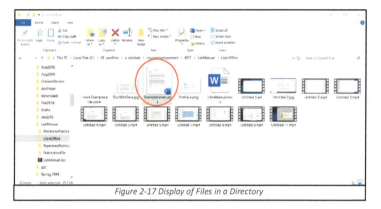

Figure 2-17 Display of Files in a Directory

If you right click on a file (preferably a .docx or .rtf or .odt file) it will open a menu of options, one of which is the "Open with" option. Clicking on the "Open with" option provides a submenu from which you can select an application to open the file (in this case we will want to use LibreOffice.)

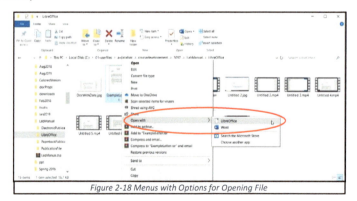

Figure 2-18 Menus with Options for Opening File

Because our example document is a .odt file, LibreOffice will choose the *Writer* application to open it (see Figure 2-19).

Figure 2-19 Example Document open in LibreOffice Writer

2.3.1 Adding an Image

A LibreOffice Writer document can include images as well as text. In our example, Mr. Jobseeker might decide that his letters should have a logo in the letterhead. With the data

entry cursor at the top of the letter, he could click on the "Insert" tab at the top of the window. This will open a dropdown menu (Figure 2-20) and one of the

options on the menu is "Image".

When Jimmy clicks on the "Image" icon a navigation window will open, and he can navigate to the directory with the desired image[10] (see Figure 2-21)

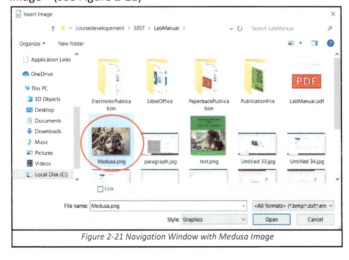

Figure 2-21 Navigation Window with Medusa Image

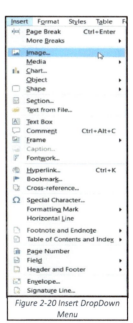

Figure 2-20 Insert DropDown Menu

---

[10] remember that Jimmy has a thing for gorgons

He would select the appropriate image and click on the "Open" button at the bottom of the window. This will insert the selected image Into the document, but not exactly where

he would want it to be located
To move the image where he would prefer to have it, Jimmy would first right click on the image and select the "Wrap" option from the dropdown menu. He would then select the "Wrap Through" option from the Wrap submenu.
With the "Wrap Through" option selected Jimmy can drag the image to the

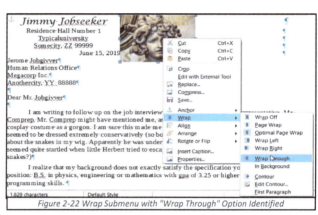

Figure 2-22 Wrap Submenu with "Wrap Through" Option Identified

position he wants it. Note that he might want to change the size of the image (by dragging one of the little corner squares inward or outward) so fit the available space.

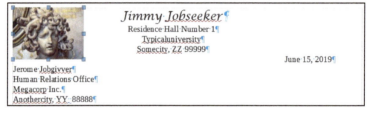

2.3.2 Bulleted Paragraphs

Mr. Jobseeker would write his followup letter substituting new text for that in the body of his original letter.

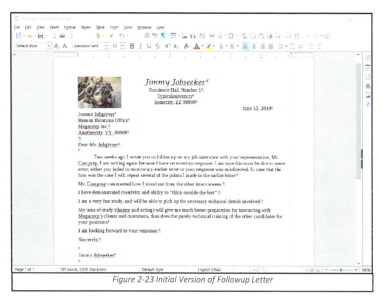

Figure 2-23 Initial Version of Followup Letter

Jobseeker might then decide that his arguments would be more effective if he were to present them in the form of a "bulleted" list.

To do this, he would first select the entries for bullets. He would then click on the "Format" tab and select "Lists" from the menu and "Bulleted List" from the resulting submenu.

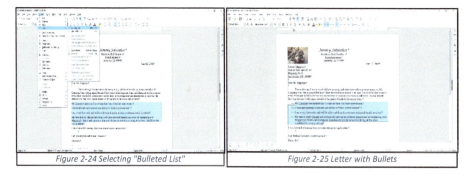

Figure 2-24 Selecting "Bulleted List"   Figure 2-25 Letter with Bullets

2.3.3 Fully Justified Paragraphs

Notice that the right ends of the lines in the main paragraph in the letter are not aligned.

If Mr. Jobseeker were to decide that he prefers the paragraph be fully justified (all lines, except possibly the first, begin in the same column and all lines, with the exception of the last) end in the same column, he would first place the data entry cursor in the paragraph in question, and then click on the "Justify" icon in the Paragraph section of the Toolbar.

Doing this will *Justify* the selected paragraph.

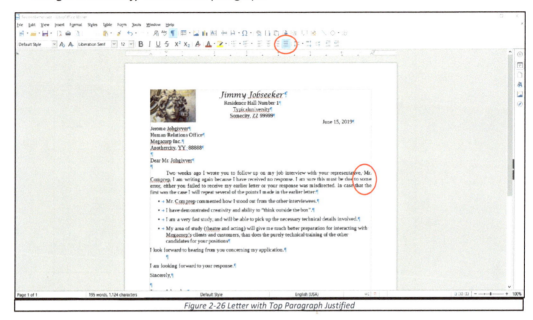

Figure 2-26 Letter with Top Paragraph Justified

2.3.4 Exercises

2.3.4.1 Write a letter that Mr. Jobgivver might send to Mr. Jobseeker in response to the letter of this section. Include a company logo and bullet list responding to each of Jobseeker's bulleted points. Save the letter in a file. Save the letter/document as a .docx file. Create an email with the letter as an attachment.

2.3.4.2 Write a letter addressed to a professor protesting a grade. Add a "School Logo" Include a list of reasons why the grade should be better. Save the letter/document as a .docx file. Create an email with the letter as an attachment.

2.3.4.3 Write a letter that a tourist agency might send a potential customer explaining why he/she/they should book a vacation with their agency. Save the letter/document as a .docx file. Create an email with the letter as an attachment.

Spreadsheets

An electronic spreadsheet is a program that allows the user to manipulate information in cells laid out in a rectangular table. A cell can typically contain a number, some text or a formula for computing values to be displayed in the cell. Spreadsheet users can adjust any stored value and observe the effects on calculated values. This makes the spreadsheet useful for "what-if" analysis since many cases can be rapidly investigated without manual recalculation.

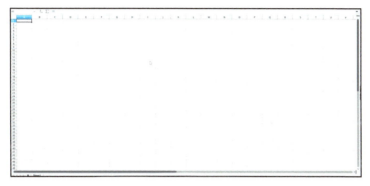

The word 'spreadsheet' came from 'spread' as with a newspaper or magazine that opens (spreads) into two facing pages, with information extending across the center fold and treating the two pages as one large page.

The compound word 'spread-sheet' came to be used to describe the format used in book-keeping ledgers—with columns for categories of expenditures across the top, invoices listed down the left margin, and the amount of each payment in the cell where its row and column intersect. The ledgers traditionally used many columns which required two facing pages, or oversized sheets of paper (termed 'analysis paper') ruled into rows and columns, approximately twice as wide as ordinary paper.

3.1 Opening a Project with LibreOffice Calc

Calc is the spreadsheet program in the LibreOffice suite.

In this project we will illustrate the construction of a spreadsheet which a professor might develop to track progress of students in a class, and, at the end of the course, compute the grades for the students.

To create the LibreOffice Calc spreadsheet, we can begin by clicking on the *"LibreOffice Calc"*

icon  to open the Calc Home window. (As shown in Figure 3-1.)

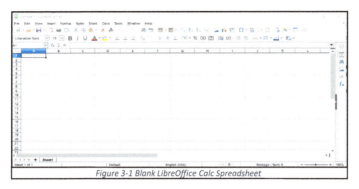

Figure 3-1 Blank LibreOffice Calc Spreadsheet

The columns in a Calc spreadsheet are identified by letters (and, for columns further to the right, multiple letters.) The rows of the spreadsheet are identified by numbers. Each cell is located in a column and in a row, and so, can be identified using a pair, a letter (or pair of letters) identifying the column, and a number identifying the row.

3.1.1 Structuring the Spreadsheet for the Class: Identifiers

In the class the spreadsheet describes, let us assume that the professor plans to will give 5 quizzes and 4 examinations. The data of each type will be stored in its own column, so we would begin the design process by entering identifiers at the top of each column: Name, Quiz1, Quiz2, Quiz3, Quiz4, Quiz5, Exam1, Exam2, Exam3 and Exam4.

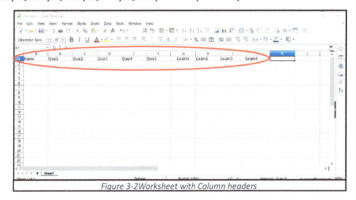

Figure 3-2Worksheet with Column headers

The student names will be entered in the left column

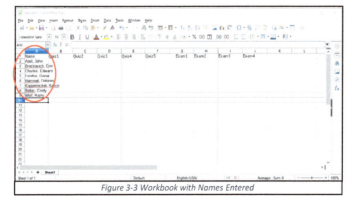

Figure 3-3 Workbook with Names Entered

You will notice (Figure 3-4) that some of the names do not fit in the default space provided in the "Name" column.

To correct this problem, we will make the space for the "Name" wider. We place the cursor at the division between column headings A and B. The cursor changes to a double  arrow.

Press the left mouse button and drag cursor to the right until the column is wide enough that all of the names fit comfortably in the space provided. (See Figures 3-5 and 3-6)

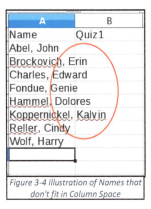

Figure 3-4 Illustration of Names that don't fit in Column Space

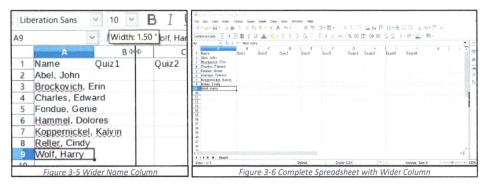

| *Figure 3-5 Wider Name Column* | *Figure 3-6 Complete Spreadsheet with Wider Column* |

3.1.3 Restructuring the Spreadsheet for the Class: Inserting a Row

Suppose, now, that another student, named Paloma Delasilla, enrolls in the class. If we want the roster to display the records in alphabetical order, her name and grades should come between those of "Charles, Edward" and "Fondue, Genie".

To insert a blank row for the Delasilla records, we would begin by selecting a cell in the Fondue row, and then click on the [icon] icon in the toolbar. A dropdown menu would appear and we would select the "Insert Rows Above" option (Figure 3-7).

This will insert a blank row into the worksheet above the row with the selected cell (Figure 3-8)

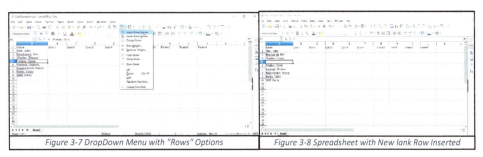

| *Figure 3-7 DropDown Menu with "Rows" Options* | *Figure 3-8 Spreadsheet with New lank Row Inserted* |

and now we can enter Paloma's name in the worksheet where it belongs.

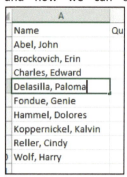

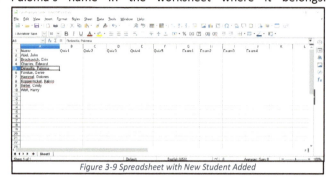

Figure 3-9 Spreadsheet with New Student Added

3.1.4 Restructuring the Spreadsheet for the Class: Inserting a Column

When the professor in charge of this class comes to assign grades, he will probably be interested in the *average* quiz scores and *average* exam scores for each of the students, rather than the scores on the *individual* quizzes and exams.

It would be natural to display the quiz averages at the ends of the lists of quizzes and the exam averages after the exam scores.

But to put the quiz averages after the quizzes, there must be spaces after the quiz scores (and before the exam scores) to display them. So, we must insert a new column between the quiz scores and the exam scores.

First, we select a cell in the column to the right of where we want the new column (i.e. we select a cell in column G, the "Exam 1" column .) Then we click on the icon in the toolbar and select the "Insert Columns Before" option from the resulting dropdown menu.

We should add a mmmmmkkkk

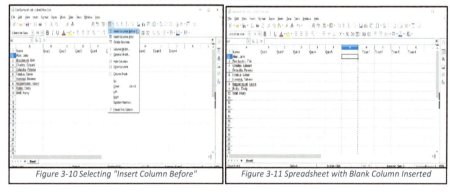

Figure 3-10 Selecting "Insert Column Before"	Figure 3-11 Spreadsheet with Blank Column Inserted

We should add a label ("Average") at the top of the new column to identify what kind of

F	G	H	
Quiz5	Average	Exam1	Ex

data will be displayed in the cells below.

3.1.5 Structuring the Spreadsheet for the Class: Inserting a Function

Of course, putting the label at the top of the column does nothing to insert averages in the cells in the column below that label.

In order to make the spreadsheet calculate the quiz score averages, we begin by selecting cell G2 (the cell immediately below the one where we put the label

"Average".)

We then click on the "Insert" tab and select "Function" from the dropdown menu.

This will open "Function Wizard" listing the available functions. We scroll down to where the AVERAGE function shows.

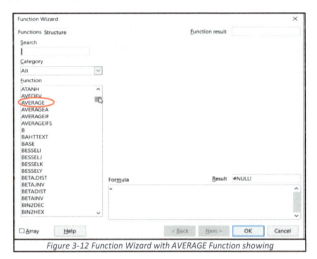

Figure 3-12 Function Wizard with AVERAGE Function showing

We double click on the AVERAGE function to open the AVERAGE function in the function

editing box.

In cell G2 we want the average of Mr. Abel's quizzes (the entries in cells B2, C2, D2, E2, and F2.) With this window open we can bring this about either by placing the cursor in B2, pressing the left mouse button and drag to cell F2. This will result in "B2:F2" being copied into the argument fields for the displays of the AVERAGE( ) function.

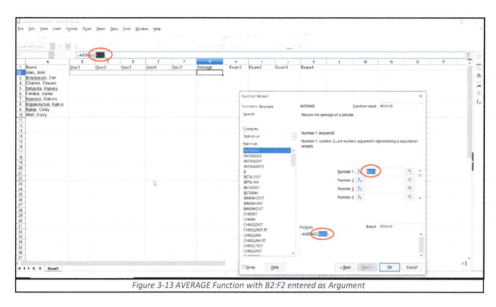

Figure 3-13 AVERAGE Function with B2:F2 entered as Argument

We could, alternatively, have entered the range B2:F2 in any of the three argument field displays.

When we click on the "OK" button, we will get an error message

The **#DIV/0!** display in the G2 cell is a "*division by zero*" error identification.

The AVERAGE function calculates the sum of the numbers to be averaged and divides by the number of nonempty entries.

In this case, there are no quiz grades (as yet) so calculating the average would involve division by zero. The error message will be replaced by a number, once the professor enters a few numbers into cells between B2 and F2.

3.1.6 Structuring the Spreadsheet for the Class: Copying Functions

The formula, at this point, only calculates the average for one student, John Abel. The professor will want the averages for all of the students. We will copy the function into all of the cells of column G.

Place the cursor on the little dot at the bottom right corner of the G2 cell.

The cursor changes form to a small + symbol.

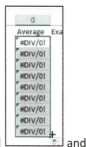

Press the left mouse button and drag the cursor down to the G10 cell and release.

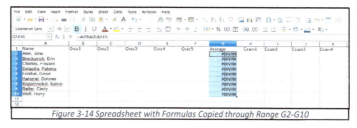

Figure 3-14 Spreadsheet with Formulas Copied through Range G2-G10

Although the function (AVERAGE) is copied into each of the cells in G2-G10, the range of values will change for each copy to reflect the row of values for which it is to compute the average. The copy of the formula in cell G3, for example, will calculate the average of numbers from B3 through F3

While that in cell B5 will calculate the average of numbers from B5 through F5.

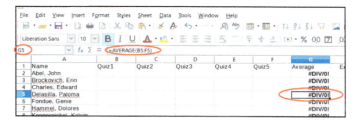

When a function references (the contents of) cells by their Column-Row identifications, then a *copy* of that function references cells with Column-Row identifications adjusted according to the position of the new copy of the function. In the case of the quizzes, the original AVERAGE function in cell G2 references other cells in row 2, the copy in cell G3 will reference cells in row 3, the copy in G4 references cells in row 4, etc.

The professor will, of course, want to calculate the averages of the exams as well as those of the quizzes, so we will have to go through the same process for column L

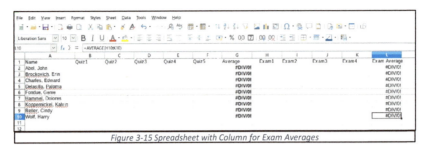

Figure 3-15 Spreadsheet with Column for Exam Averages

The professor might well be interested in the relative difficulty of his quizzes, and so would want to calculate the average scores in each of the individual quizzes. To calculate these, we might begin by entering a label (Quiz Average) in Cell A12, and then, with cell B12 selected, we once again select the AVERAGE function. Next we would place the cursor on cell B2, press the left mouse button and drag the cursor down to B10.

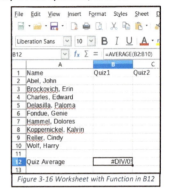

Figure 3-16 Worksheet with Function in B12

This, structures the spreadsheet to calculate the average scores of the quiz 1. Now we place cursor on the dot on lower right corner of B12, press left mouse button and drag to F12, to copy the AVERAGE function into the cells B12 – F12.

The new copies of the AVERAGE function will have column identifications adjusted, just as the row numbers were adjusted when we copied the functions calculating student quiz averages into new rows (see Figure 3-17).

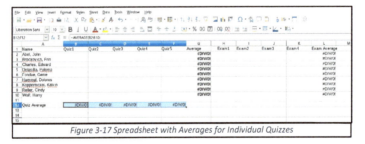

Figure 3-17 Spreadsheet with Averages for Individual Quizzes

3.1.7 Structuring the Spreadsheet for the Class: Inserting a User Defined Function

We will assume that the professor in the course has announced that the quiz average will count as 10% of the final grade in the course and the exam average will be counted 90% of the final score, he would now like to have a function to compute these final course grades.

There is, of course, no "built-in" function that will calculate 10% plus 90%, so we will have to create one.

We select a column for the course average (Column N) and enter an appropriate label at the top (in cell N1). Then, in the cell below it (cell (N2) we enter =0.1*G2+0.9*L2

Notice that, as we enter the text in cell N2, it also appears in the formula bar.

When the content of a cell begins with the = symbol, what follow will be a formula/function and the value it produces when evaluated is what will be displayed in that cell. (Please note that in each of our AVERAGE functions, the first symbol in the cell is the = symbol)

In such a formula/function, the numbers from other cells are referenced using the column-row identifications of the cells and the arithmetic operations are identified using the following symbols:

- +   indicates addition

- -   indicates subtraction

- *   indicates multiplication

- /   indicates division

In the above example, a function was created (the entry begins with the symbol =) The function multiplies the number displayed in cell G2 by 0.1 (calculating 10% of John Abel's quiz average) and multiplies the number displayed in cell L2 by 0.9 (calculating 90% of his exam average) and adds the two products.

Click on the "Enter" check mark to confirm the entry in L2

Now we put the mouse cursor on the dot at lower right corner of the N2 cell, press the left mouse button and drag down to cell N10 to copy the function into the rows corresponding to the other students (with appropriate adjustments to cell references in the formulas[11].)

---

[11]   Copying formulas by dragging downwards will produce increasing row numbers in the copies of the formulas. Dragging to the right will cause column references to increase (A to B, B to C, etc.)

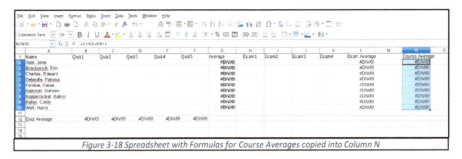

Figure 3-18 Spreadsheet with Formulas for Course Averages copied into Column N

After the professor has entered quiz and exam grades, the spreadsheet might look something like Figure 3-19 below.

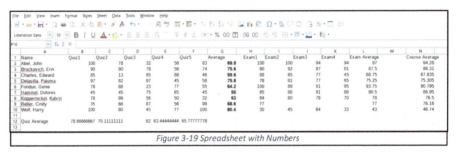

Figure 3-19 Spreadsheet with Numbers

3.1.8 Saving the Spreadsheet

The process of saving a LibreOffice Calc spreadsheet is essentially the same as that of saving a LibreOffice Writer document.

If the spreadsheet has been saved previously, and we were saving a revised copy (with the same filename) then we would only have to click on the "Save" icon in left part of the toolbar.

If, on the other hand, the spreadsheet has never been saved (or if we want to save the current version with a new name to differentiate it from earlier versions) then we begin by clicking on the "File" tab in the upper left corner and then select the "Save As" option from the resulting dropdown menu. This will open the "Save As" window, where we an navigate to the directory where we want to save the new file (or file with new name.) Then we enter the desired file name in the "File Name" entry box. (see Figure 3-20)

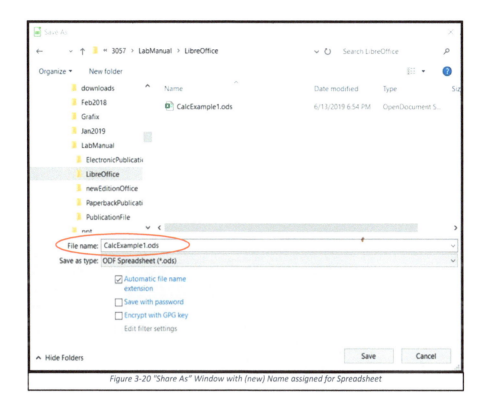

Figure 3-20 "Share As" Window with (new) Name assigned for Spreadsheet

3.1.9 Exercises

3.1.9.1 Create a "shopping list" spreadsheet, with, in one column a list of names of items to be purchased, in another column, the number of the items purchased, in a third column the price[12] per unit of each item, and in a fourth column the total amount spent on that item (computed with a user defined function.) At the bottom of this column should be the total bill.

(This kind of spreadsheet might be installed on a mobile device, and the user could fill in item names, numbers and prices while shopping, and it could compute what his/her bill should be before arriving at the cashier.).

3.1.9.2 A car dealership sells several different models of cars. All cars of a given model have the same value/price.

Create a spreadsheet for the dealership, showing in one column, the names of the models, in another column the values of the models, in a third column the number of cars of each model currently on hand at the dealership, in yet another column the total value of all the cars available of the given model, and in still another column the number of recent sales of cars of that model. There should also be a column with the total values of recent sales of cars of the models. Finally, in a row beneath all of that, the spreadsheet should show total value of all cars on hand and the total value of all recent sales.

3.1.9.3 Create a spreadsheet that would calculate the "Grade Point Average" for a student.

In one column would be listed the courses that the student took. In a second column the number of credits of each course, and at the bottom, the total number of credits in all courses. In a third column his/her grade (numerical) in each course. In a fourth column the product of grade and credit value for each course, and at the bottom, the sum of all of those products. Finally, in another cell (labelled GPA) the quotient, the sum of the products divided by the sum of the credits.

---

[12] To display the number in a cell with a currency format (as a number of dollars and cents) select that cell and click the "Format as Currency" icon ⬚ in the spreadsheet toolbar.

3.2 Reformatting a LibreOffice Calc Project

The Calc spreadsheet we created in project 3.1 calculates and displays the desired values, but it doesn't make it easy for the viewer to distinguish between the computed averages and the individual quiz/exam scores.

Calc provides a number of facilities for making spreadsheets look better and convey information more effectively.

3.2.1 Representation of Decimal Values

Notice (Figure 3-21) that the values computed as "averages" in the example spreadsheet appear with widely varying numbers of decimal digits, some with none, some with one digit, some with two, even some with up to 8 digits.

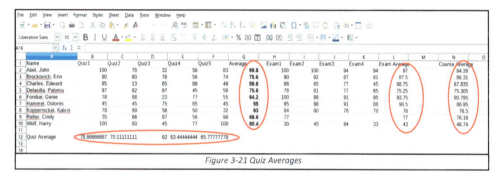

Figure 3-21 Quiz Averages

The spreadsheet would look better if the decimal formats were more consistent.

The LibreOffice Calc toolbar includes several icons for formatting displays of numbers.

If we select the "Quiz Average" values and then click on the "Format as Number" icon (0.0) the quiz average display format will change to a two digit decimal format:

| 78.67 | 70.11 | 62.00 | 63.44 | 65.78 |

We can use the various icons in sequence to set the displays to number of digits we want.

Figure 3-22 Quiz Averages and Decrease Decimal Icon

3.2.2 Insertion of New Column

The spreadsheet displays all of the numerical values in columns of the same width and, with the exception of the Course Average column, in columns that are adjacent.

Because they are so close together, it is difficult to distinguish different types of information.

It seems reasonable for the data for exams to be separated from that of the quizzes. We can do that by selecting a cell in the Exam 1 column then clicking on the "Column" icon in the toolbar .and select the "Insert Columns Before" option from the dropdown menu. (see Figure 3-23)

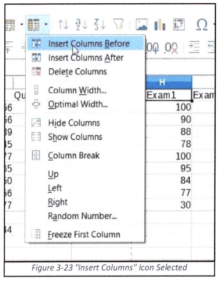

Figure 3-23 "Insert Columns" Icon Selected

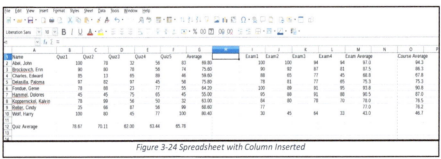

Figure 3-24 Spreadsheet with Column Inserted

3.2.3 Alignment and Widths of Columns

The labels in the headings over the columns with numerical values do not align well with the numbers. The numbers are "right aligned" while the labels are left aligned.

We can change the label alignment by first selecting the labels, and then clicking on the "Right Align" icon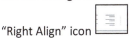

The result is pretty good, except for columns L and M where the M column is not wide enough to hold the entire label.

Figure 3-25 Labels Right Aligned

To fix this problem, we place the cursor at the right edge of the "M" cell and press the left mouse button. The cursor changes to a double arrow ↔. Then we drag the edge to the right, enlarging the column to the point that the labels do not interfere with each other.

3.2.4 Chart Displaying Data

To help a user visualize data in a spreadsheet, Calc provides many sophisticated tools to create graphic displays for data representation.

In this situation of this example, the professor might be interested in a display to illustrate the relative difficulty of the quizzes.

We could start by selecting the data to be represented (the quiz score averages) and the identifiers (the quiz labels at the top)

	Quiz1	Quiz2	Quiz3	Quiz4	Quiz5	Ave
	100	78	32	56	83	
	90	80	78	56	74	
	85	13	65	89	46	
	97	82	97	45	58	
	78	88	23	77	55	
	45	45	75	65	45	
	78	99	56	50	32	
	35	66	87	56	99	
	100	80	45	77	100	
	78.67	70.11	62.00	63.44	65.78	

Figure 3-26 Averages and Labels

and then we click on the "Insert Chart" icon in the toolbar

This will open the "Chart Wizard" from which we can choose the type of chart to use.

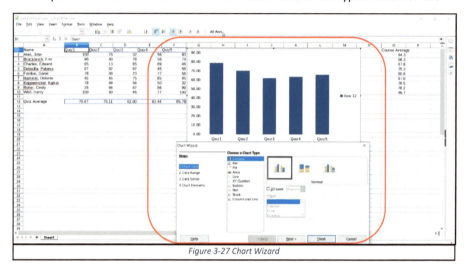

Figure 3-27 Chart Wizard

We After selecting the chart type, we click on "Finish" and drag the chart to the position where we want it.

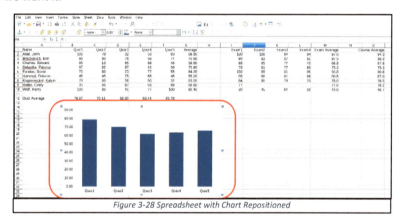

Figure 3-28 Spreadsheet with Chart Repositioned

3.2.5 Exercises

3.2.5.1 Create a spreadsheet showing: in one column the names of (at least 4) baseball teams, in a second column the number of games played by the teams, in another column the number of runs scored by the teams, and in yet another column the number of runs scored per game by the teams (expressed with three decimal digits of accuracy.)

Below the numbers there should be a graph showing the runs per game for the teams.

3.2.5.2 A car dealership sells several different models of cars. All cars of a given model have the same value/price. Create a spreadsheet for the dealership, showing in one row, the names of (at least 4) car models (do not put a model name in column 1.)
In row 2, under each model name should be the price of that model.

Below the model/price display should be:
In column A, a list of the names of (at least 4) salesmen.
In the column for each model, in the row for each salesman should be the number of sales of that model of car by that salesman.
In the column to the right of the last car model should be the total values of the sales for that salesman. There should also be a graph displaying the total value of sales by each salesman.

3.2.5.3 Create a "shopping list" spreadsheet. Along the top row should be a list of recipes. Down the left column should be a list of items to be purchased.
In the row for an item, under each recipe should be the number of units of the item needed for the recipe. Then, to the right of the recipe entries should be an entry for the price per unit of the item, and another entry for the total amount to be spent on that item.
In a row beneath all of the items should be entries for the total amount to be spent on the recipe of each column.
Finally there should be two graphs, one displaying the cost of the recipes and the other showing the amounts spent on the items.

Presentation Programs

A **presentation program** is a software package used to display information in the form of a "*slide show*".

Presentations like this are widely used in business communications, (especially in business planning) as well as in education and, generally, anywhere ideas are to be communicated. Presentations may also feature prominently in political settings where persuasion is a central motivating issue.

A presentation program is supposed to help both the speaker and the participants/viewers. It will provide visual information which complements the talk. There are many different types of presentations including professional (work-related), education, entertainment, and for general communication.

The presentation program included in the LibreOffice software suite is called Impress.

4.1 Opening a Project with LibreOffice Impress

To start an Impress project, we begin by (double) clicking on the Impress Icon to open the Impress "Home" window.

4.1.1 Impress "Home" Window

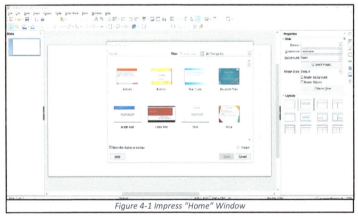

Figure 4-1 Impress "Home" Window

The Home window provides a number of icons for templates (*themes*) for new Impress projects. Choosing one of these themes results in a presentation display in which each slide has a similar color background and design. The simplest, however, is the blank presentation, which we open by clicking on the "Cancel" button. (default title "untitled 1". See Figure 4-2)

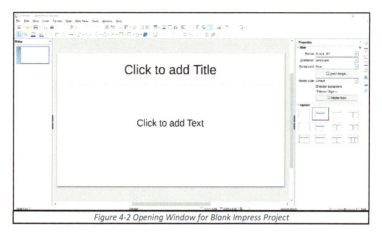

Figure 4-2 Opening Window for Blank Impress Project

4.1.2 Initiating the Project

A professor might want to create a sequence of PowerPoint slides to supplement his lecture on the first day of a class.

4.1.2.1 Title Slide

The first slide in the display will be formatted as a title slide (an area at the top where the title for the slideshow might be entered, and another area below where explanatory text can be entered[13].)

The professor would probably use this initial display to identify the course he would be talking about.

He/we would enter this information where the slide says "Click to add Title" and "Click to add Text".

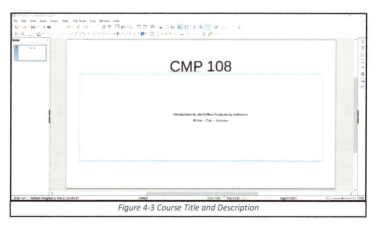

Figure 4-3 Course Title and Description

---

[13]   If you fail to enter anything in a region labelled "**Click to add …**" it will appear in blank during slideshow display.

4.1.2.2 Text Properties

The text sizes shown in Figure 4-3 do not match, the lower entries are too much smaller than the upper ones, and are probably difficult to read..

We can adjust the text properties by:

First selecting the text to be dealt with

Next selecting the "Properties" icon ⬚ in the right sidebar.

This will open the **Properties** dialog box (Figure 4-4)

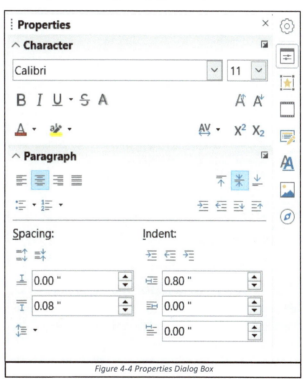

Figure 4-4 Properties Dialog Box

One of the properties we can reset from this dialog box is the "Font Size"

A size of 28 would be more appropriate than 11 (see Figure 4-5)

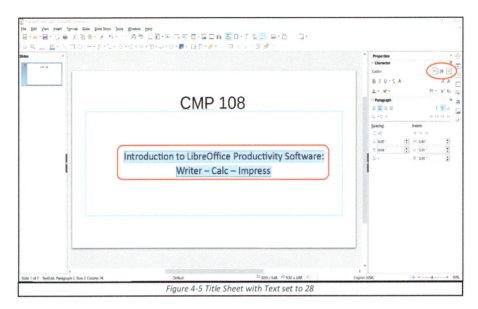

Figure 4-5 Title Sheet with Text set to 28

4.1.3 Outline of Lecture

Recall that this "Slideshow" (like most slideshows) will be displayed as the professor talks. It should show points of emphasis and details that should be remembered. It would *not* be a word for word repetition of what he will be saying.

The professor will probably begin by introducing himself.

Next, he would give a brief general outline of the course

Then a very brief description of each of the primary topics: Writer, Calc and Impress

4.1.4 Slide for Professor Introduction

Our project will need a slide to supplement the professor's self introduction: We can click on the "Slide" tab in the toolbar and select the "New Slide" option from the dropdown menu[14] (Slide 4-6)
The default slide layout for new slides is the title and content layout (as in Figure 4-7)

Figure 4-6 Slide Menu

---

[14] Or we could simply press Ctrl-M, as indicated in the menu

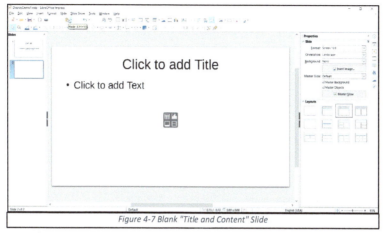

Figure 4-7 Blank "Title and Content" Slide

We would enter an appropriate "Title" for the first slide in the presentation:

By default, the entries in the "Content" block will be displayed in "Bullet" format:

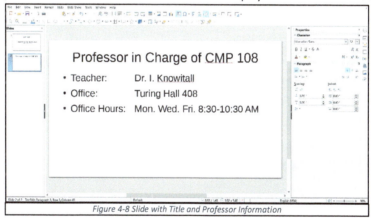

Figure 4-8 Slide with Title and Professor Information

4.1.5 Slide for Course Description

Right clicking on the "Professor Introduction" slide icon in the left column will open a window with a menu. One of the menu options is "New Slide".

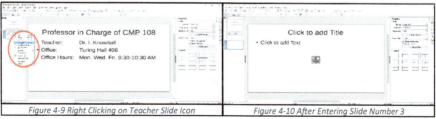

| *Figure 4-9 Right Clicking on Teacher Slide Icon* | *Figure 4-10 After Entering Slide Number 3* |

Then we enter the title and information describing the course:

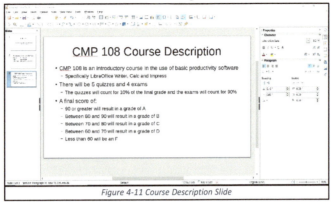

Figure 4-11 Course Description Slide

The entries in "Bullet" format can be inset using the *tab* key (normally the key marked "→")

4.1.6 Slides for Course Content

The lecture would also include a short description of each of the LibreOffice programs to be studied: Writer, Calc and Impress. Each would have its own slide, and each of the slides would be created the same way that the "Course Description" slide was created; right click on an icon in the left column, select "New Slide" from the dropdown menu, and then edit the resulting slide.

Figure 4-12 Slides for Writer, Calc and Impress

4.1.7 Slide with Image

It seems reasonable that the professor should also tell the students what the textbook for the course is. He would do this with a slide immediately following the one with the course description.

We select that slide and then click on the down arrow of the "New Slide"

icon on the toolbar 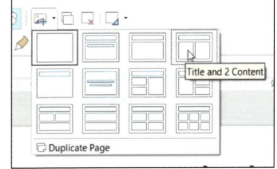. This produces a dialog box with several alternative slide layouts. We will select the "Title and 2 Content" option, giving us something like Figure 4-13, below.

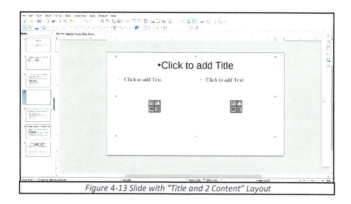

Figure 4-13 Slide with "Title and 2 Content" Layout

We next click on the "Insert Image" icon [Insert Image] in the left "Content" section and, in the "Insert Image" navigation window we locate the directory with the image of the textbook, select the image and click on the "Open" button.

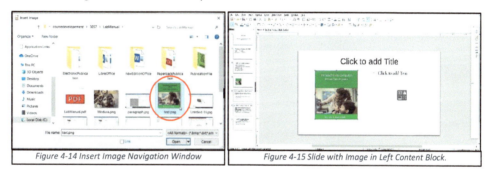

Figure 4-14 Insert Image Navigation Window   Figure 4-15 Slide with Image in Left Content Block.

We can adjust the size and position of the image by selecting it and dragging the small square "handles" that appear at its corners. Then we enter a title for the slide and text describing the book in the content block on the right hand side of the slide.

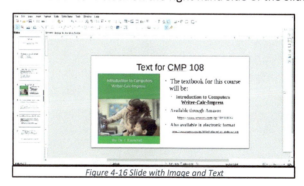

Figure 4-16 Slide with Image and Text

4.1.8 Exercises

4.1.8.1 Create a presentation similar to that in the example above for a course that you are familiar with. The presentation should have at least 5 slides. It should have a teacher self introduction page which includes an image of the teacher. (This is *presumably* a *fictional* course with a *fictional* teacher, so do not feel constrained by the truth, but DO take into consideration the laws governing libel and defamation of character.) The presentation should use one of the *theme*s mentioned in section 4.1.1

4.1.8.2 Create a presentation that a (fictional) salesman might use in promoting the sales of (fictional) vacation packages. The presentation should have at least 5 slides, it should have a theme applied and at least one of the vacation package descriptions should include an illustration.

4.1.8.3 Create a presentation that will explain/show how to prepare a dish like ZucchiniSpaghetti (see Chapter 1)

4.2 Dynamic Impress Presentations

The slide show developed in the previous section has a simple display format. Every time the presenter clicks his/her mouse button or presses a key, the current slide immediately disappears, and is replaced by the next slide (in its entirety.)

This is kind of transition is quite adequate for a short sequence like our example, but for a longer lecture with numerous slides, it can quickly become boring.

Impress provides a number of techniques for making the presentation more dynamic, and helping keep the audience awake and interested.

4.2.1 Transitions

The "Slide Transitions" dialog box gives us a number of options for "transitioning" from one slide to the next.

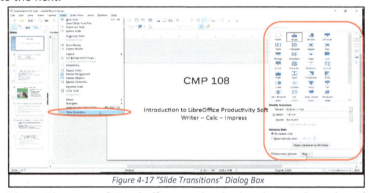

Figure 4-17 "Slide Transitions" Dialog Box

These provide a wide range of visual effects as the display changes from that of one slide to the next.

A "Transition" effect is applied to a slide by simply clicking on the effect icon while the slide is in the editing window.

If, with slide #2 showing in the editing window, we click the "Uncover" icon and set "Modify Transition" Variant to "Top to Bottom"

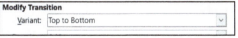

then the transition from slide #1 to #2 will proceed as shown in Figure 4-18 below.

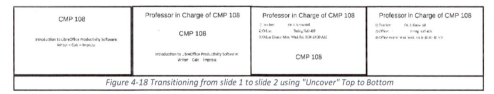

Figure 4-18 Transitioning from slide 1 to slide 2 using "Uncover" Top to Bottom

4.2.1.1 Selecting the Transition

Impress provides a large selection of transition effects. The reader is cautioned to keep in mind that the function of the presentation is normally to supplement a lecture. Overutilization of transition effects has the potential of distracting the audience's attention from the lecture.

You would be better advised to avoid the more spectacular effects and choose subtle variations of relatively common transitions.

4.2.2 Animations

Now we have some (hopefully) interesting visual effects as presentation transitions from one slide to another. Impress also provides tools to support additional display "Animations" on individual slides.

We access these animations by clicking the "Animations" entry in the "Format" dropdown menu. This opens the "Animation" dialog box.

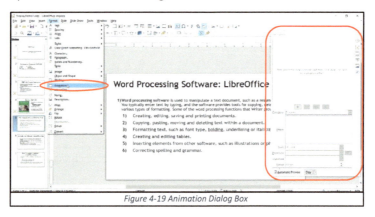

Figure 4-19 Animation Dialog Box

Possibly the most common use of these "Animations" is to display objects one at a time as the presenter talks about each of them in turn.

Dr. Knowitall might, for example, feel that, when discussing the "Creating, editing, saving and printing documents" aspect of LibreOffice Writer (the first entry in the list of functions provided) it would be distracting to have the lines concerning "Copying ...", "Formatting ...", etc. on the screen too. He might like to talk about one set of functions, then have another line appear so he could talk about those functions, then have another line appear so he could talk about its functions, and so on.

Word Processing Software: LibreOffice Writer

1) Word processing software is used to manipulate a text document, such as a resume or a report. You typically enter text by typing, and the software provides tools for copying, deleting and various types of formatting. Some of the word processing functions that Writer provides are:

1) Creating, editing, saving and printing documents.
2) Copying, pasting, moving and deleting text within a document.
3) Formatting text, such as font type, bolding, underlining or italicizing.
4) Creating and editing tables.
5) Inserting elements from other software, such as illustrations or photographs.
6) Correcting spelling and grammar.

4.2.2.1 Starting the Animation

With slide 5 (the Writer slide) displayed and the "Animation" dialog box open, we select the object for the first animation effect
the line "1) ...

and click on the  button in the dialog box.

This will add the first animation effect on the slide (initial entry in the

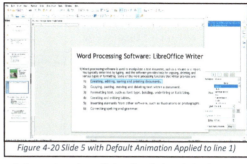

Figure 4-20 Slide 5 with Default Animation Applied to line 1)

animation list – the rectangle at the top of the animation dialog box) the default animation as applied to the selected object. The default animation is for the object to appear when the mouse button is clicked

Category – Entrance
Effect – Appear
Start – On Click

We next select the second object we will want to appear
Line "2) ...

and click the button

This will add the second animation effect on the slide (second entry in the animation list.) Again, the default animation is applied to the selected object

Figure 4-21 Slide 5 with Default Animation Applied to line 2)

We can continue, selecting lines and applying the default animation to each of them (See Figure 4-22.).

With the slide configured in this way, when Dr. Knowitall comes to the point in his lecture where he will discuss word processing, slide 5 will initially display only the title and the initial paragraph (either of which have been assigned animations. See Figure 4-23)

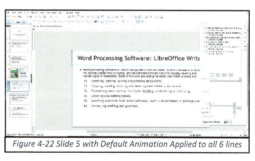

Figure 4-22 Slide 5 with Default Animation Applied to all 6 lines

When he feels it would be appropriate, Dr. Knowitall could click the mouse button (or press a key on his computer keyboard) and line number one will appear (Figure 4-24.)

When he is done talking about line 1, he can click again, and line 2 will appear (Figure 4-25)

When he clicks again, line 3 will appear (Figure 4-26)

And the next click will display line 4 (Figure 4-27)

And similarly, mouse clicks will display lines 5 and 6 (Figures 4-28 and 4-29.)

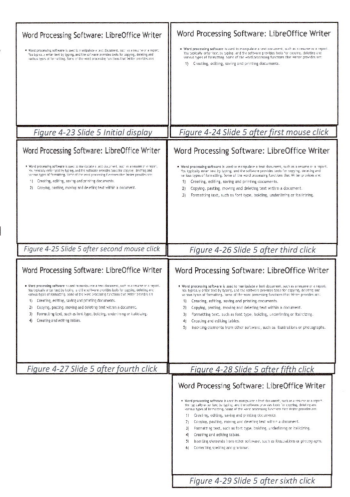

Figure 4-23 Slide 5 Initial display

Figure 4-24 Slide 5 after first mouse click

Figure 4-25 Slide 5 after second mouse click

Figure 4-26 Slide 5 after third click

Figure 4-27 Slide 5 after fourth click

Figure 4-28 Slide 5 after fifth click

Figure 4-29 Slide 5 after sixth click

4.2.2.2 Animating Objects and Choosing Effects that can be Applied

In our example, all of the animation effects are the default (simplest) effect, an object (a line of text) appearing when the mouse button is clicked.

There are, of course, very many other animation effects.

"Animated" objects are not restricted to lines of text. Images (and other kinds of objects as well) can also be animated. Dr. Knowitall might, for example, prefer that, on slide 4, the image of the text be displayed only after the title of the book has been announced.

Objects can also disappear from the display (Category "Exit", as opposed to the default "Appear".)

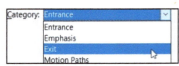

Objects can also fly in to their desired positions from various directions (or out from them), fade in (or out) or come to (or from) normal state using various visual effects.

Effects are not restricted to being "triggered" by mouse clicks. They can also be programmed to occur immediately after the animation that appears above them in the animation list.

("Start - After previous")

They can also be programmed to occur at the same time as the animations listed above them

("Start - With previous")

4.2.2.3 Choosing Animation Effects

As with transitions, animation effects can be overutilized. The effect should support the lecture. More impressive visual effects should be used to call attention to points in the presentation, not just to look impressive. They should be used to support the presentation and should not distract from it.

4.2.3 Exercises

4.2.3.1 Create a presentation similar to that in the example in the text for a course that you are familiar with. The presentation should have at least 5 slides.
The teacher's self introduction page should include an image, a picture of the teacher.
As in Exercise 4.1.8.1, this is *presumably* a *fictional* course with a *fictional* teacher. You need not feel constrained considerations of reality. (You should, however, take into consideration copyright laws, as well as those governing libel and defamation of character.)
The image of the teacher should "Fly in slow" into view upon the first mouse click. .

4.2.3.2 Create a presentation that a (fictional) used car salesman might use. The presentation should have at least 5 slides, each describing a different car, its features, price and financing terms. The different elements of the slides should be "Animated" appropriately to support a sales presentation.

4.2.3.3 Create a presentation that will explain/show how to bake a cake. Use "animation" to emphasize the sequence in which the different steps must be carried out.